On the cover
LOUISE ROBINSON BARN Cedar County,
near Mechanicsville. (More information on page 22.)
Photo by Don Poggensee

Heritage on the Prairie

This book was published by the Iowa Barn Foundation, a
non-profit, primarily all-volunteer group founded in 1997
and dedicated to preserving Iowa's barns. The group has
raised funds from individuals, foundations, and corpora-
tions to give to private property owners to preserve their
barns so important to Iowa's agricultural heritage.

Owners of some of the barns pictured in this book
have received grants from the Iowa Barn Foundation.
Some owners have been given awards of distinction by
the foundation for being rehabilitated at their expense.
All of the photographs are of Iowa barns, beloved and
cared for by owners.

The photographers, editor, writer, and assistants who
contributed to this book were all volunteers dedicated
to saving important symbols of Iowa's agricultural heritage.

Editor: Jacqueline Andre Schmeal

Essay Writer: Ober Anderson

Assistants:
Andrea Corcoran
Don Geiger
Carrie Jones
Tom Lawler
Ray McFarland
Roxanne Mehlisch
Richard Schmeal
Jeffrey Fitz-Randolph

Special Assistant:
Roxanne Mehlisch

Photographers:
Ober Anderson
Kenneth Dunker
Duane Fenstermann
Marlene Fenstermann
Jeffrey Fitz-Randolph
Don Poggensee
Sue Robinson
Ken Starek
Wilford Yoder

Printer:
J&A Printing, Hiawatha, Iowa

For information on this book, the Iowa Barn Foundation,
or to order this book, please call foundation secretary,
Roxanne Mehlisch, at 641-487-7690.

HISTORY OF
IOWA
BARNS

By Ober Anderson

For over 300 years, from 1650 to 1950, the American all-purpose barn, usually the most prominent building on a farm, was the center of hard work focused on making a livelihood from raising crops and animals. So important was the barn that it was often built before the house. Sometimes the family lived in the barn until the house was built.

Early Iowa barns often reflected the nationality of early settlers. Some, like the Norwegian barns in northeast Iowa, were adapted from barns left behind in Europe. Bank barns built into the side of a hill or bank, so upper and lower floors could be accessed from the ground level, were adapted from European barns. Barns in Marion and Sioux Counties, many hip-roofed, reflect the Dutch heritage of the area.

While ethnic barns were built in eastern Iowa with its rising dairy industry in the 1880s, prairie or western barns on open grassland farms, such as cattle feeder barns, met a farmer's need there to feed and shelter cattle that they fattened for shipping by rail to slaughterhouses. Prairie barns which began dotting the western half of Iowa after the Civil War, increased greatly in numbers during the 1880s, and continued to be built through World War II. These large barns often housed livestock on the lower level and had storage for hay on the second level. Others had feed bunks surrounding the barn's center that were filled with hay piled from the floor to the roof. Both varieties had a large door at the roof peak for loading hay into the loft with a hay fork that raised hay from the farm wagon up to a hay carrier, fixed to the peak, which could pull the hay inside.

The oldest barns in Iowa are in the eastern part of the state—some pre-Civil War. Eastern Iowa had plentiful wood for building barns of heavy timber framing—then the common barn construction method for connecting timbers with wooden pegs. Using local timber and rocks from the property, early settlers built the size of barn they could with available local help and the time they could give to it. Later, as farm wealth accumulated, some farmers hired skilled barn builders who used wood that had been floated by river from Wisconsin and Minnesota to Mississippi River mills for sawing and shipment by rail.

Until there were rail connections for bringing in sawed lumber, community saw mills prevailed. They were often operated by a local farmer who took a portable horse-powered saw to a building site. As time went on, farmers created their own barn designs, incorporating ideas taken from *Des Moines Iowa Homestead* or *Wallace's Farmer, Chicago Prairie Farmer or Breeders' Gazette.* Additional designs also came from the Iowa State University's agricultural engineering department and the United States Department of Agriculture.

Early settlers usually selected their home sites near timber and water. Timber was needed for firewood as well as construction of homes and buildings. In central and western Iowa, timber was not always found in large supply. Often timber was purchased from a neighbor. Sometimes early families purchased small timber lots of five to 20 acres. The Ballard Country Club, Huxley, sits on one of these sites.

When a barn was in the finishing stage of construction, families gathered together for a "barn raising" when lots of energy was needed to lift the rafters into place. After the barn was completed, a barn dance was held on the floor of the hay loft. Family members and neighbors from miles around joined in fun, food, and fellowship. Barns also played an important role in the social life of a farm family. It was a place for play and for basketball.

Barns continued to be constructed until shortly after World

War II. Then, following the rapid mechanization during the war and better all-weather roads, which enabled farmers to drive their modern machinery to numerous farm parcels they owned or rented, the overall size of these fragmented farms nearly doubled between 1900 and 1950 and has persisted. Thus, there are fewer farms and barns. Fewer families live on the land. No longer do farmers raise a variety of livestock where a relatively small number for horses, beef cows, dairy cows, sheep, and hogs might occupy a single barn. As farm families became employed off the farm, larger specialized buildings were erected for each type of livestock. The first of these were the large, caged layer buildings holding several thousand laying hens in one house. Larger dairy and beef cattle barns followed. Once swine diseases were under control, large hog confinement buildings followed. This efficiency of scale allowed for less labor and ultimately less expensive food for the consumer.

The historic Iowa barn is a rapidly diminishing resource. At one time there were over 200,000 barns in Iowa. It is estimated the some 50,000 remain.

Fortunately, for barn enthusiasts and historians, many farmers are willing to ignore profitability in the interest of tradition and

heritage to maintain their barns. The Iowa Barn Foundation is dedicated to making this possible through their grant programs, tours, and resources for barn restoration.

It is important that Iowans save historic barns. The historic barn offers us a sense of place as a "Cathedral on the Prairie."

Some have said that, next to the American flag, barns are one

A barn in the winter.
Photo by Wilford Yoder

of the most recognized symbols of our national history, America's work ethic, the American dream.

Built by untrained "artists", they are folk art just as quilts are.

Most of the barns in this book are still standing. Some are gone, but they were important enough to be featured in a book about Iowa barns. Each had a role in Iowa's history-in America's history.

Ober J. Anderson grew up on a crop and livestock farm in Winnebago County when, sometimes, they milked cows by lantern light. He graduated from Iowa State University in agricultural education in 1958 and later got a master's degree. He spent a 35-year career working in the Iowa State Agricultural Extension Service. Later he worked in farm management and appraisal where he conducted over 500 farm appraisals. He always took note of the barns and has been active in the Iowa Barn Foundation since its beginning and often lectures about barns.

BARNS OF
NORTHEAST IOWA

Emery Bridge Barn, Winneshiek County, combines an internal bridge found in most Norwegian barns with post and beam building methods of nineteenth century American barns. Barn was built between 1871 and 1906. (3453 Bear Creek Road, Decorah) *Photo by Kenneth Dunker*

Gribble Barn, Winneshiek County, was built by Michael and Rose Puffer, immigrants from Czechoslovakia, for their Brown Swiss dairy herd around 1900. The barn has remained in the family. (3109 155th Street, Fort Atkinson) *Photo by Marlene Fenstermann*

Kolsrud Barn, Clark Kolsrud was dedicated to saving this family's fifth generation Norwegian barn near Waukon. The 30x50-foot barn was built by John Jacobson. The family bought the land in 1862. He spent five years building the barn. (1243 Gjefle Drive, Waukon) *Photo by Marlene Fenstermann*

Kruger Barn, Allamakee County, proud dairy barn was built in 1915 and has been in the same family for some 60 years. (310 Northline Drive, Waukon) *Photo by Duane Fenstermann*

Log Barn, Allamakee County, was built in 1868 and was as primitive then as in 2005 when it was taken down. At one time 15 cows were kept in the barn. Owned for many years by the Asleson family.
Photo by Kenneth Dunker

Thomas Reburn Barn, was built by a
traveling crew in 1914. It is twelve-sided.
(1641 Pool Hill Drive, New Albin)
Photo by Kenneth Dunker

BARNS OF
EAST CENTRAL IOWA

Amana Barns, Iowa County, contributed to the character of the Amana Colonies, once a commune of 1800 persons. The barns inside the villages were built in the manner of European barns where people lived in towns and went out each day to work the land. These barns are larger than most because of the communal farming practices. The barns feature heavy timber, pegged construction, and hand-hewn and mortise and tenon joinery. West Amana bank barn, 130x46, was built in 1886 and has two doors on the bank side. *Photo by Wilford Yoder*

Smith Barn, Dubuque County, was built in 1917 and has been in the same family since then. Jack Brehm, 28, prepared the frame over the winter prior to construction. Beams were precut and holes for pins were drilled. The crew slept on the lawn during the week. (90922 Asbury Road, Durango) *Photo by David Kettering*

The Fields Barn, built in the 1870s by William and Charles Fields, Cedar Falls bankers, for their thoroughbred horses and Holstein cattle, was one of the most distinguished barns in Iowa. The magnificent limestone barn was a traffic stopper, but the traffic stopped when the barn was taken down in 2008. The barn was described in 2008 Waterloo Courier: *"A pile of rubble is all that remains of an historical Cedar Falls stone barn. The structure, built in the 1800s, came down with little fanfare last week, despite years of protests by many community preservationists"* (Barn was west of Cedar Falls on Highway 57) *Photo by Don Poggensee*

Coyner Barn, Muscatine County, was built in the late 1800s when bricklayers came through the area and built houses and barns including this one with unique bricks. (2304 Highway 22, Muscatine)
Photo by Wilford Yoder

DeFries Barn, Jackson County, is 47x84 feet
and was built in 1885 by A.B. DeFries
whose family settled in the area in the
1850s. It is post and pegged construction.
(17929 232nd Avenue, Maquoketa)
Photo by Don Poggensee

Dighton Barn, Delaware County, was built in 1914 by Rob Kirkpatrick, a farmer, who was obsessed with round barns. Hollow tile was shipped from Chicago. A bricklayer worked six days a week for three months for $195. Work was done with handsaws, broad axes, and hammers. The final cost was $1997. The intricate barn is on the National Register of Historic Places. (3344 120th Avenue, Coggon)
Photo by Kenneth Dunker

Dirks Barn, Jones County, was built in 1888 by Charles Bates and measures 40x64 feet. Added onto in 1891, it is now 40x100 feet and has a wing measuring 16x24 feet. The barn is of mortise and tenon beam construction. It has a stone foundation held in place by mortar. Lumber for the barn came from nearby timber. (12913 County Road E 17, Scotch Grove) *Photo by Don Poggensee.*

Driscoll Barn, Cedar County, was built in 1875. The pre-cut and pre-drilled segments of the barn were delivered to Mechanicsville during the winter, loaded onto bob sleds, and carried five miles to the farm. The barn was assembled on the farm during the spring. (641 Dixon Avenue, three miles south of Mechanicsville)
Photo by Don Poggensee

Fiddelke Barn, Delaware County, sits on Coffin's Creek, west of Manchester. The area called Coffin's Grove was settled in 1840. The Fiddelke barn was raised July 4, 1849. (1337 Candle Road, Manchester)
Photo by Don Poggensee

Gehlen Barn, Jackson County, sits in the middle of St. Donatus, a historic Luxembourgish village. It was arguably built in 1839 making it one of the oldest barns in Iowa.
(101 North Main Street., St. Donatus)
Photo by Don Poggensee

McNutt Barn, Johnson County, was built in 1918. The beams are pegged mortise and tenon construction. Ed Kader's signature and the year 1918 are visible in the concrete floor. (3021 White Oak Avenue, NE, Iowa City)
Photo by Wilford Yoder

Ostrem Barn, Johnson County, was built 1940 with native oak lumber from the barn site. Beams are pegged mortise and tenons. The barn has a Dutch style gambrel roof with southern exposure over-hanging roof line for weather protection to animals and the doors in the lower level. The extended gable peak is for mounting the hayfork track and getting hay through hay door into the haymow. The barn is used for horses and has horses inside. (4631 Kansas Ave SW, Iowa City) *Photo by Wilford Yoder*

Prison Industries South Barn, Jones County, is one of
the Romanesque Revival style barns associated with
the Anamosa State Penitentiary. The barns were built
of ashlar limestone quarried nearby. The South barn,
built in 1912, is a side-hill barn with the main floor
opening directly into a hillside and the basement
level centered on the downhill side. (Barn can be
viewed from County Road E 28, west of Anamosa)
Photo by Sue Robinson

The Ridden-Hahn Barn, Delaware County, dates back to the English settlement of the 1850s around Dyersville. It was built by William Ridden. During the 20th century it was owned by the Hahn family. The limestone barn features keystone limestone arched doors.
(One mile west of Dyersville)
Photo by Don Poggensee

Louise Robinson Barn, is a 72x46 bank barn built by Jeremiah Baughman, who moved to Cedar County from Pennsylvania in 1862. It is believed the barn was built with timbers floated down the Mississippi. The date, 1880, is inscribed on the oats bin. The cupolas have red stars on four sides suggesting the Red Star Route, a shipping route that went between Muscatine and Cedar Rapids. (493 Fox Avenue, Mechanicsville) *Photo by Don Poggensee*

Scheer Barn, Linn County, was built in 1881 and has interior wooden silo. Barn named for original maple grove that surrounded log cabin before barn built. (3386 73rd Street, Fairfax) *Photo by Don Poggensee*

Schemmel Barn, Dubuque County, sits on land homesteaded in 1867. The barn was built in 1871 from lumber taken from the area. Anton Schemmel, the original owner, born in 1850, was one of the first native Iowans of European decent born in the state. (29998 Rockville Road, New Vienna)
Photo by Don Poggensee

Schneckloth Barn, Scott County, was built by Herbert Schneckloth, prominent Iowa farmer, whose family emigrated from Germany in 1854 and built this landmark round crib in 1926. Work on the 50-foot diameter structure was done with hand tools. The foundation was dug and poured by hand using a shovel and one-third a bag of home mix at a time. (2353 200th Avenue, Davenport) *Photo by Jeffrey Fitz-Randolph*

Schiele Barn, Cedar County, this landmark barn in Cedar County was home to renowned Herefords. (2132 Vermont, Durant)
Photo by Ken Starek

Muscatine Barn, formerly owned by the Stein family, was built as a dairy barn in 1924 for $3000. (2975 Highway 22E Muscatine) *Photo by Don Poggensee.*

Stromeyer Barn, Jackson County, is a beloved well-cared for historic family farm. A historic pioneer cemetery can be seen from the barn. (37647 Iron Bridge Road, Spragueville) *Photo by Don Poggensee*

Thompson Seven Springs Barn, Muscatine County, has some double walls for warmth. (2094 Seven Springs Road, Muscatine) *Photo by Kenneth Dunker*

Tjaden Barn, Jones County, was built in 1912 and painted green with paint supplied by a Minnesota vendor. It was subsequently painted green and is consequently a landmark. (9956 Highway 64, Wyoming)
Photo by Kenneth Dunker

Weber Barn, Jackson County landmark barn, was built in 1928. (Highway 52, north of St. Donatus)
Photo by Don Poggensee

BARNS OF
SOUTHEAST IOWA

Altmaier Barns, Johnson County, was built in
1885. (3294 480th Street, SW, Iowa City)
Photo by Wilford Yoder

Bartelt Barn, Des Moines County, a peg and post basement barn with a limestone foundation, was built in the 1870s. The main oak hand hewn support beam is 12x14x40 feet long. The barn is 40x70 feet. (16296 Highway 61 seven miles south of Mediapolis)
Photo by Don Poggensee

Galloway Barn, Van Buren County, was built prior to 1887 for W.A. Barker, a livestock producer. It was larger than other barns in the area measuring 40x62 feet. Oak logs, hewn beams (12-inches x 12-inches), and milled lumber were used in construction. The beloved and historic barn was lifted and crashed to oblivion by a 2018 tornado. (16677 Highway l, Keosauqua)
Photo by Jeffrey Fitz-Randolph

Johnson County Home Barn, was on 160 acres the county supervisors bought outside Iowa City in 1855 as a "poor farm" to provide care for needy individuals. Still intact is a brick cistern outside the barn. (4515 Melrose Avenue, Iowa City) *Photo by Kenneth Dunker*

Maasdam Barns, Jefferson County, was owned from 1910 to 1938 by Jacob Maasdam, who raised and sold champion Percheron draft horses. The Mare Barn, built in 1910, is a gable roof structure that is 28 feet long and 18 feet wide. The barn was equipped with Louden overhead monorail hay carriers, first developed and manufactured by Louden Machinery Company, in nearby Fairfield. (2000 South Main Street, Fairfield)
Photo by Jeffrey Fitz-Randolph

Parsons Barn, Van Buren County, is a 36x42-foot board and batten barn, built about 1870, on a limestone foundation. The lower level livestock area on the south features open forebay in the Pennsylvania tradition. Lower level interior walls are limestone. (22055 Highway, Keosauqua) *Photo by Jeffrey Fitz-Randolph*

Piping Hollow Corn Crib, Des Moines County, was built in 1916, by Thurmand A. Dotson with tile made in Newport, a quarter of a mile north of the structure. The 20-foot diameter crib held 1400 bushels of ear corn. It was filled via a wooden elevator that took four men to put up to the crib. The crib showed how tile could be used for corn storage.

Photo by Don Poggensee

Roberts Barn, was one of the most photographed barns in America. The two-story octagonal barns stands on a foundation 14 to 16 inches thick. Each of the eight sides is 26 feet long. The barn is 61 feet in diameter. The Roberts family settled in the area about 1860. (4716 Kansas Avenue, SW, Iowa City)
Photo by Don Poggensee

Sleichter-Rhodes Barn, Johnson County is a Pennsylvania style barn with posted bays opposite the ramp to the second floor. It is one of the oldest barns in Johnson County. Lumber used for the building came down the Mississippi to a sawmill in Muscatine.(5648 Kansas Avenue, Riverside)
Photo by Wilford Yoder

Strabala Barn, Washington County, was built in the 1920s. (930 290th Street, Washington)
Photo by Don Poggensee

BARNS OF
NORTH CENTRAL IOWA

Hansen Corn Crib, considered one-of-a-kind, was built in the 1940s and holds 7000 bushels of ear corn and, in the center of the crib, storage for 4000 bushels of small grain. (401 40th Street, Ruthven) *Photo by Don Poggensee*

Haugen Barn, Winnebago County, was built in 1915.
In 1924 Peter Haugen enlarged it using a handsaw
to split the barn in two. He added to the middle.
(18446 420th Street, Leland)
Photo by Kenneth Dunker

Iowa Falls Barn, a huge and magnificent barn that was burned.

Photo by Don Poggensee

Klousia Barn, Franklin County, was built in 1888. It has a limestone foundation with wooden peg construction. The lower level is a walkout basement to the east. The middle section had stanchions for milk cows and the north side held three calf pens. (1766 165th Street, Hampton) *Photo by Kenneth Dunker*

McBurney Barn, Humboldt County, was built in 1890 on land owned by Stephen Taft, who founded Springdale, which became Humboldt. In 1874 he sold the land to Lorbeers who built the house and barn, which has been actively used and cared for through the years. (2550 Gotch Park Road, Humboldt) *Photo by Kenneth Dunker*

Rockefellow Barn, Mitchell County. Stunning northern Iowa bank barn with limestone foundation, built in 1877 for horses and cattle. (4480 Echo Avenue, St. Ansgar) *Photo by Kenneth Dunker*

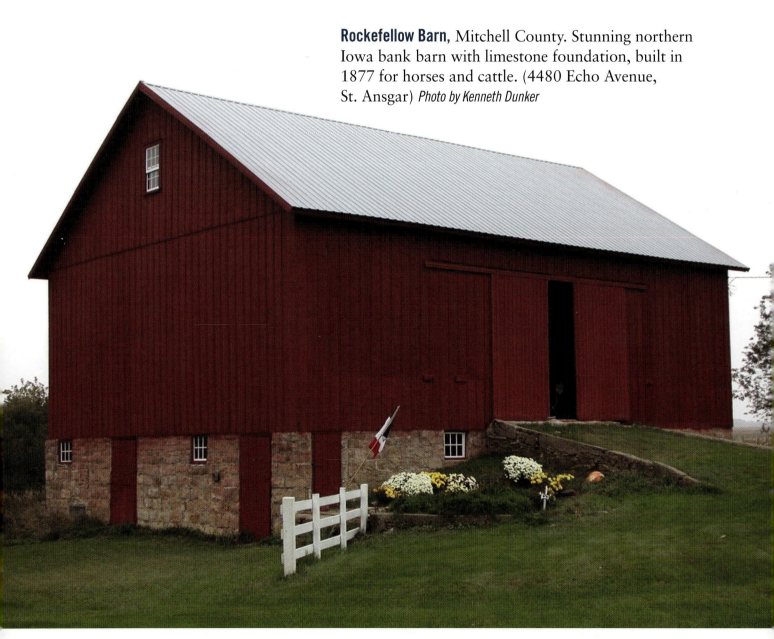

Younker Barn, Butler County, has been in the same family since 1875. A landmark barn, it is 112 x 30 feet. "Stella Younker Cox, Sinclair, IA" is stenciled on each board. The 2008 Parkersburg tornado took trees on the farmstead and left the important barn unscathed. (25734 Highway 57, Parkersburg)
Photo by Kenneth Dunker

BARNS OF
CENTRAL IOWA

Buck Barn, Marshall County, shows the beauty of a restored small barn in central Iowa. Inside the barn is a cupola bell. (1271 285th Street, State Center)
Photo by Kenneth Dunker

Dobbin Barn, Marshall County, 65-feet in diameter, was built in 1919. It was a pre-cut structure made to order by Gordon Van Tine, Davenport. It has a 12-foot diameter clay silo with 13 dairy cow stanchions, five double horse stalls, two box stalls, grain rooms, milk and tack rooms. (2551 Brown Avenue, State Center)

Interior photo by Kenneth Dunker
Exterior photo by Ken Starek

Handsaker Barn, Story County, is a handsome square barn built in 1875 on land purchased by the Handsaker family in 1853. The family gave land for the town of Fernald.
Photo by Don Poggensee

The Hayward Round Barn, Tama County, is 66 feet in diameter. It was built in 1916 on land purchased by the family in 1881. It was challenged after a tornado hit it, but Loie Hayward restored her historic family treasure. (1520 V 37 Dysart)
Photo by Don Poggensee

Iowa State University Horse Barn, Story County, was designed by distinguished Des Moines architects, Proudfoot, Birds and Souers, known for buildings throughout the Midwest including the Wichita courthouse. The barn was built between 1923 and 1926 and has striking metal ventilators and lightning rods. The haymow covers the entire building. (University Avenue and Stange Road, Iowa State University campus) *Photo by Kenneth Dunker*

Jefferson Highway Barn, Hardin County, sits on the remnants of the historic Jefferson Highway, founded in 1915 and went from Winnipeg to New Orleans. Often people camped in the yard. The barn was designed and built by August Saaksmeier after the turn of the century. (2915 JJ Avenue, 1.5 miles south of Hubbard)
Photo by Ken Starek

Pfantz Barn, Marshall County, was built by August Riemenschneider in 1902. Balloon framing was used in building the barn with two interior posts to support the four-gable roof and massive cupola. (210 4th Avenue, State Center)
Photo by Kenneth Dunker

O'Rourke Pioneer Barn, is a basement pegged barn. The Mulcahys,who were from Ireland, purchased the land on which the barn was built in 1872. The barn remained in the family until 1999. The barn is on the National Register (25623 710th Avenue, Colo)
Photo by Kenneth Dunker

Brekke Barn, Story County, was built by Addison Kingsbury. (6020 East Lincoln Way, Ames) *Photo by Don Poggensee*

Richards Barn, Greene County, is one of the original buildings on The Thornburg Home Place. (2201 R., Jamaica)
Photo by Kenneth Dunker

Rosenfeld Barn, Story County, was built in 1918 and has 27 four-paned windows for light and ventilation. It is 90x66 feet. It housed a nationally recognized purebred herd of Aberdeen-Angus cattle. (520th Street, Kelley) *Photo by Kenneth Dunker*

Wittern/Hubbell Barn, Polk County, a grand and magnificent barn (36x144 feet), was constructed in the 1920s by Fred W. Hubbell, who used the barn for his "blue ribbon" shorthorn cattle raised on the 1200-acre farm. (Army Post Road, Des Moines) *Photo by Ober Anderson*

BARNS OF
SOUTH CENTRAL IOWA

Weitl-(Beeler) Barn, Dallas County, was built in a German settlement by the Burger brothers including one who became the first county agent in Iowa. (2569 140th Street, Van Meter)
Photo by Kenneth Dunker

Blake Barn, Clarke County, is a landmark barn on I 35 seven miles south of Osceola. It was built in 1902 by folks whose roots were in England. (2155 Benson St., Weldon) *Photo by Kenneth Dunker*

McBroom-Hargis Barn, "would be the largest barn in this part of the country" stated the Madison County paper in 1884. It has a wooden track, post and pegs. It was designed by I.F. Carter of DeSoto. 1218 Highway 169, Winterset (Madison County) *Photo by Kenneth Dunker*

Harken-Oswald Barn, Clarke County, was designed in the 1930s and could be converted into a show pavilion to seat over 700. Farm was operated with the thought of helping the small producer market his animals. (1071 Harken Hills Drive, Osceola) *Photo by Don Poggensee*

BARNS OF
NORTHWEST IOWA

Ackerman Barn, Osceola County, built about 1915,
is 84x36 feet and has remained in the same family.
There is a "matching" hog house that is 56x34 feet.
(Corner of L-58 and Highway 9, north of Ocheyedan)
Photo by Carrie Jones

Beldt's Broadview Ranch Barn, Lyon County, was built on land bought by Prussian immigrants, Charles and Christine Beldt, in 1882. The barn is 48x80 with a foundation of red granite brought into the county by rail and horses. (2572 Log Avenue, Sheldon) *Photo by Ken Starek*

Booth-Kirschner Barn, Clay County, was built in 1890 by Philip Kirschner on land that has been in the family since 1856. Pictured is the distinguished widow's walk around the cupola – arguably one of the only ones in the state. (North of Peterson at the top of the hill, then west)
Photo by Carrie Jones

Conover Barn, Ida County, was built about 1900 and used by C.B. Conover and his son, C.B., Jr., for their outstanding Belgian draft horses. Iowa Secretary of Agriculture, Harry Linn, used to give draft horse demonstrations at this barn. (5315 190th Street, Holstein)
Photo by Don Poggensee

Hoffman Barn, Plymouth County, was built at the turn of the century by Theodor Hoffman. The land, on which the barn sits, was homesteaded by Dennis Hoffman in 1870. Most of the wood used in building the barn came from cottonwood trees on the farm. The barn was the scene of many barn dances. Lawerence Welk played at some of those dances. South of LeMars in Plymouth County. *Photo by Don Poggensee*

Jones Barn, Osceola County, was built in 1916 and has been in the family for generations. (Verdin Avenue in Ocheyedan)
Photo by Carrie Jones

Otto Barn, Osceola County, was built in the 1880s by Mennonites from Canada, who settled in the area in 1887 and left for Pennsylvania in 1915. The pegged barn's haymow holds 10,000 bales. Livestock was kept in the lower level of the barn. (One-half mile east of May City on 225th Street) *Photo by Don Poggensee*

Le Mars Barn, Plymouth County. When H. A. (Peter) Tonsfeldt designed this round barn in 1918, he wanted a structure to show off his Polled Hereford bull and pure-bred cattle. The 51 foot silo in the center is anchored six feet below and creates a self-supporting building. At one time the farm was offered at auction and was eventually donated for the Plymouth County Fairgrounds. (500 4th Avenue NE, Le Mars) *Photo by Don Poggensee*

Lorch Barn, Osceola County, Mennonite barn built in 1889, has distinctive overhanging side. (220th Street and M-18)
Photo by Don Poggensee

BARNS OF
WESTERN IOWA

Dunham Barn, Crawford County, built in 1870, is considered one of the earliest brick barns in western Iowa. The bricks were fired at a kiln northwest of the barn. The walls of the barn are four bricks thick at the lower level and three bricks thick at the upper level There is a 40-foot hand-hewn walnut beam in the lower level. (Highway 37 one mile west of Dunlap) *Photo by Don Poggensee*

Ellis Barn, Calhoun County, is known by locals as "the big red barn". Built in 1918, the 36x80-foot barn is 40 feet high to the eaves and has 3x12-inch timbers. Shirley and Larry Ellis bought the farm in 1971 and have used their barn for Arabian show horses.(2370 Fletcher Avenue, Lytton) *Photo by Kenneth Dunker*

Sessions Barn, Monona County, is on what is called by locals, "the model farm". The farm buildings were constructed in a Gothic style 1936 by James McIntyre who used plans provided by Iowa State University Midwest Plan Service. The two barns are connected which is not typical. (233275 280th Street, Onawa) *Photo by Don Poggensee*

Waveland Barn, Ida County, was a National Register round barn, 50 feet in diameter, built in 1900. It had vertical siding and large central section with a cone roof. It went on the National Register in 1986 and was bulldozed in 2010. *Photo by Don Poggensee*

Finken Barn, Logan. This barn built in 1917 on land that has been in the family since 1892. The roof has laminated rafters which were raised into place with gin pole and horses. Each rafter is five boards thick, bolted together, and cut into curved shape.
Photo by Kenneth Dunker

BARNS OF
SOUTHWEST IOWA

Clarinda Mental Health Institute Barn, a three-story, one-of-a-kind horse barn was believed to have been built around 1905. The facility started out with seven horses. By 1930 there were 32 horses and mules. Horses were obviously considered when building the barn, as it is dotted with windows that brought light to the animals which were worked by patients. (1800 N. 16th Street, Clarinda)
Photo by Kenneth Dunker

Clarinda Mental Health Institute Heifer Barn, is where, at one time, 3000 pounds of milk were needed daily. There is room to milk 100 cows. The total Holstein herd including calves, heifers, bulls, and dry cows averaged 270. *Photo by Don Poggensee*

The Lake Barn, Page County, was built by D.S. Lake, a horticulturalist from New Hampshire, who brought fruit stock with him when he came west to set up a nursery. The barn for the Lake Nursery Barn was built in 1870. Lake Nursery influenced many other nurseries in the area which came later. Restoration efforts came too late. *Photo by Kenneth Dunker*